The Ultimate Medicare Decision Making Formula

A Consumer's Guide to Medicare Supplement, Medicare Advantage, and Part D Plans

———————— ————————

by
DAN BROOKS

Copyright © 2013 Dan Brooks

All rights reserved.

ISBN: 1484943759

ISBN 13: 9781484943755

The information included in this book reflects the opinion of the author. Although every attempt has been made to verify all facts cited, I will not be held responsible for any mistakes, misstatements, inaccuracies, or omissions. This information is neither approved nor endorsed by the Centers for Medicare and Medicaid Services, the Department of Health and Human Services, or any other federal agency. Only by understanding the unique circumstances of any individual situation can a specific recommendation for any insurance coverage or plan be made.

Introduction

The purpose of this book is to help you, the new Medicare beneficiary, make a swift and accurate decision in regard to your Medicare health plan choices. I will take you through the process step by step, removing the confusion, stress, worry, and information overload that might overwhelm you as you consider this decision. Use the fast and accurate formula provided here to avoid feeling forced into choosing a health plan. This book will give you the information that you need to successfully complete this process, including:

- How to avoid common mistakes when choosing a Medicare plan
- How to differentiate the various parts of Medicare
- How Medicare works with employer group insurance
- How to decide what form of Medicare best fits you
- How to quickly and efficiently find the best plan
- How to identify the benefits that you actually need

The information presented here is borne out of over fifteen years of experience as an agent in the Medicare plan marketplace. Over that time, I have developed an internal, proprietary process as a result of thousands of hours of meetings with people just like you, people who need guidance, direction, and knowledge in order to make a well thought-out health plan decision. As a professional in the Medicare insurance field, I have helped thousands of people decipher the complex information available. I know that I can also help you to make a swift and accurate plan choice. If you follow the steps presented here, I promise that you will quickly and accurately find the right Medicare health plan—one that not only meets your personal health care needs but also your lifestyle and your budget. In fact, I guarantee it as I have been using this formula for years with complete success. If you employ all of the strategies described here and complete all of the worksheets included, you will absolutely be able to make an educated plan choice.

Now for the bad news, when I said that this process is simple, I meant it. Completing the steps to do so, however, is not necessarily easy. If you promise to do the background work required, then I promise to enable you to make a wise Medicare plan choice. The effort that you put forth will help to maximize your time and energy associated with this process. Additionally, once you've made your decision, you will have a clearer understanding of the plan selected, giving you the security of knowing that you made an educated choice.

There will be many Medicare terms used throughout this material. A glossary of definitions is provided in the back for reference.

CONTENTS

Chapter One:
Getting Started 1

Chapter Two:
Forms First...7

Chapter Three:
Count Your Health Care Assets and Untangle Your Employer
Group Insurance..13

Chapter Four:
Identify the Benefits You Need 19

Chapter Five:
An Overview of Original Medicare Benefits..................................25

Chapter Six:
Understanding Medicare Supplement Policies 31

Chapter Seven:
Understanding Medicare Advantage Plans 41

Chapter Eight:
Understanding Medicare Part D and the Doughnut Hole 47

Chapter Nine:
Getting Extra Help from Federal, State, and Local Sources..........53

Chapter Ten:
Optimizing Your Medicare Benefits 57

Chapter Eleven:
The Value of an Agent..59

CHAPTER ONE:

Getting Started

What is Medicare?

Medicare has been around since 1965 when Congress passed the Social Security Act, which included the provision of health insurance to people over the age of sixty-five. Since that time, social security has expanded to include eligibility for younger individuals with permanent disabilities or people diagnosed with end-stage renal disease (ESRD). Other changes include privatization of administrative duties to private insurance companies.

Today, the general rules for Medicare eligibility are five-year residency in the United States plus ten years spent working and paying Medicare taxes. If you meet these guidelines, you are eligible for Part A and Part B of Medicare. Further, Part A is provided to you at no cost. If you did not work, you can still qualify through your spouse. Other qualifications apply for disability, ESRD, and amyotrophic lateral sclerosis (ALS) patients.

Medicare Coverage Overview

Medicare consists of four parts. *Part A* includes hospital insurance and covers inpatient stays in hospital as well as skilled nursing facilities. Other services covered under Part A take place in the home. These include home health care and hospice care.

Part B is the medical insurance portion of Medicare. It includes services provided by doctors and other health care providers. Outpatient care and *durable medical equipment (DME)* are also covered under Part B as well as some preventive services.

Part C, also known as *Medicare Advantage*, consists of medical plans administered by private insurance companies. These plans include all of the services and benefits covered under Part A and Part B. Medicare Advantage Plans usually includes a drug benefit (*Part D*) and can include extra benefits not typically covered under Medicare. Additional premiums may be associated with Part C plans.

Part D constitutes the prescription drug component of Medicare. These plans are also administered by private insurance companies and can significantly lower your out-of-pocket cost for prescription drugs.

The default means by which to get Medicare is referred to as *Original Medicare*. Original Medicare consists of Part A (hospital) and Part B (medical). If you want prescription drug coverage, you must add Part D, a *prescription drug plan* or *PDP*. If you want supplementary coverage beyond the basic Medicare, you have the option of adding a *Medicare supplement* or *Medigap* policy. To view a short video outlining the basics of Medicare, visit my website http://medicareplanchoice.com.

Starting Medicare and Making Adjustments

Whenever you make changes to your Medicare—including initial enrollment—it's necessary to have a valid *election period*. An election period is like a permission slip from Medicare that allows you to make changes or adjustments to your Medicare benefits. Medicare does not physically provide you with anything to indicate that you have an election period. Instead, they assume that you know the rules including the time frames available to use them. Your first election period is called the *initial coverage election period* or *ICEP*. During the ICEP, you may begin to receive Medicare benefits pending eligibility by age or by disability.

When Can You Sign Up for Medicare?

You can sign up for Medicare as soon as you become eligible for Part A and/or Part B during your initial enrollment period. If you're eligible because of age at sixty-five, you can sign up at any point within the seven-month window illustrated below. As shown, the sign-up period begins three months before you turn sixty-five, includes the month in which you turn sixty-five, and ends three month after you turn sixty-five.

Initial Coverage Election Period

3 months before you turn 65	2 months before you turn 65	1 month before you turn 65	The month you turn 65	1 month after you turn 65	2 months after you turn 65	3 months after you turn 65

Getting Started

In order for your benefits to start the month of your sixty-fifth birthday, you must sign up within the three-month window prior. If you delay signing up until the month of your sixty-fifth birthday, your benefits won't begin until the month following. The same is true for the second and third month following your birthday; benefits will kick in the month after you sign up. If, however, you wait to sign up until the fourth month following the month of your birthday, your benefits can be delayed further. At this point, you will need to wait until *general enrollment*, which occurs January 1 to March 31 each year. In this case, your benefits will begin in July and you may have to pay a higher premium for late enrollment.

If you are currently collecting Social Security, you are automatically enrolled in Medicare. If you are not yet collecting Social Security, you must apply for Medicare benefits either by going to a Social Security office, enrolling online at socialsecurity.gov, or enrolling by phone at 800-772-1213.

How Much Will I Pay for Part A and Part B?

As discussed previously, as long as you have met the qualifications for Part A, the cost to you is zero. Most people pay the standard premium ($104.90 in 2014) for Part B. However, if your modified adjusted gross income as reported on your IRS tax return from two years prior is above a certain amount, you will pay more. The following chart shows the premium amounts.

2014 Part B Premium Chart

Filed Individual Return	Filed Joint Return	File Married & separate Return	2014 amount
$85,000 or less	$170,000 or less	$85,000 or less	$104.90
$85,001 to $107,000	$170,001 to $214,000	N/A	$146.90
$107,001 to $160,000	$214,001 to $320,000	N/A	$209.80
$160,001 to $214,000	$320,001 to $428,000	$85,000 to $129,000	$272.70
$214,001+	$428,001+	$129,001+	$335.70

Late Enrollment Penalties

Late enrollment penalties or *LEPs* occur when you don't take certain Medicare benefits (specifically Part B and Part D) when you are first eligible to do so. First, let's discuss Part B. To avoid the Part B penalty, make sure that you sign up for Part B during the period discussed above. Alternatively, you may delay enrollment in Part B if you are covered by an *employer group health plan* (*EGHP*) through your own employment or that of your spouse. In this case, you will not be penalized as long as you sign up for Part B while the EGHP coverage is still active or during the eight-month period following EGHP coverage or employment termination (whichever occurs first). If you are penalized for late enrollment in Part B, you must pay 10 percent more for each full twelve-month period that you delayed enrollment in addition to the regular premium amounts.

COBRA

The Consolidated Omnibus Budget Reconciliation Act (known more commonly as COBRA) was passed by Congress in 1986 to allow employees to temporarily keep employer-provided health insurance benefits after employment ends or after a loss of coverage from a spousal employer. It's important to understand that COBRA is not considered an EGHP or coverage through a current employment. This means that if you wait until your COBRA plan ends and you wait more than eight months following your Medicare eligibility date, you may be subject to LEP for Part B. Therefore, if you choose COBRA, do not wait until your COBRA coverage ends to enroll in Part B.

Affordable Car Act Plans

If you are enrolled in an *Affordable Care Act* (ACA) plan prior to becoming eligible for Medicare, you should be aware of a few items. ACA plans are not designed to work as Medicare Supplement or Part D coverage. It is possible to keep the ACA plan however there can be implications. First any tax credits or premium reductions are immediately cut off. Secondly, Medicare Part B penalties can still occur. You can choose an ACA plan if you're eligible for Medicare but have not enrolled either because you would need to pay the Part B premium or you are not yet collecting Social Security. Doing so however could again subject you to future Part B penalties as well as limiting your enrollment period to only the *general enrollment period*. It is also against the law for anyone to offer you an ACA plan if they know you are already on Medicare.

ACA plans that are provided by employers follow the same general rules as regular employer coverage. If you're covered by an employer ACA plan based on you or your spouse's current employment, you can still apply for your Part B benefits without penalty during the eight month window after the employment ends or the coverage ends (whichever happens first).

Other Medicare Election Periods

There are additional common election periods of which you should be aware. The *annual election period* or *AEP* runs each year between October 15 and December 7. During AEP, you can add or subtract Part D and/or change your status between Original Medicare and Medicare Advantage.

The *Medicare Advantage Disenrollment Period* (or *MADP*) is held between January 1 and February 14. During this period, you are able to drop the Medicare Advantage Plan in order to return to Original Medicare. During MADP, you can also add Part D should you revert back to Original Medicare.

Finally, Medicare allows several *special election periods* or *SEPs*. SEPs allow changes to be made in response to certain circumstances. The most common include moving out of the service area of a Medicare Advantage plan, eligibility for the *Extra Help* prescription assistance provided by Social Security, eligibility for state medical assistance or *Medicaid*, and eligibility for a *state pharmaceutical assistance program* (*SPAP*). We will refer back to some of these terms in later chapters.

This chapter described when and how to enroll in Medicare as well as how to make adjustments in the future. To be sure you gleaned important points, ask yourself a few questions. Do you know if you be automatically enrolled in Medicare or will you need to apply for benefits? Do you know when you can sign up for Medicare? Do you know how much you will be paying for Part B Medicare? The next step is to understand the choices you have when initially accepting your Medicare benefits.

CHAPTER TWO:

Forms First

You might be dreading the process of choosing a Medicare plan. Examining materials from different companies and trying to make sense of it all might just seem like a hassle. You might be thinking that choosing your Medicare plan could be one of the biggest decisions you make. I would argue that it is an important decision, but selecting the plan is ultimately less crucial than the form of Medicare that you decide to take. If you do the necessary planning in advance, you'll make the right decision and will choose the form of Medicare that works best for you. Choosing the best plan within the right form of Medicare is often easier than one might think. Simply match up your benefit and premium needs with the plans available. I'll show you how including step-by-step directions over the next two chapters.

When deciding what form of Medicare to choose, you immediately come to a fork in the road. Deciding which way to go at this stage will help you to see more clearly the plan that's right for you. It will also help to eliminate many of the other plans, saving you time and frustration. Medicare states that there are two distinct ways to receive Medicare benefits: Either through Original Medicare or through a Part C Medicare Advantage Plan. Original Medicare would be the default way, and would consist of Parts A and B of Medicare. You have the option to add to this a Prescription Drug Plan PDP for prescription drug coverage and or a Medicare supplement or Medigap policy.

A Medicare Advantage plan would be the second alternative to receiving your Medicare benefits. An important part of this Medicare decision philosophy is the ability to understand the differences between these two options and to be able to identify the benefits and drawbacks of each as they apply to your individual circumstances. Though you don't need an in-depth understanding of insurance, you do need a deep enough understanding of the two forms of coverage to keep from getting confused. Without this know-how, it's easy to become overwhelmed by the choices available.

We'll cover the differences between the two forms of Medicare again in detail later, but for now, let's look at the two possible combinations. Medicare's most basic explanation is this: You can have Original Medicare with Part D and/or Medigap options or you can have Medicare Advantage with PDP options—but not both. The following chart shows the two separate tracks you can take.

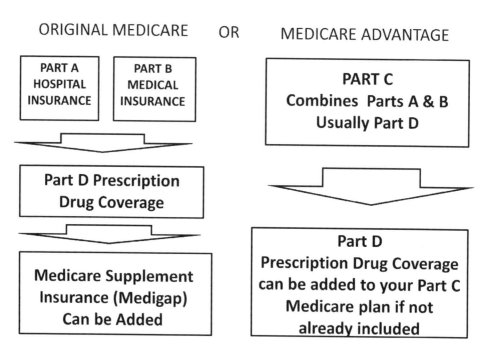

The primary difference between the two forms of Medicare is how the claims are processed. When a claim is processed through Original Medicare, the doctors and hospitals send the hospital claims to Part A and the medical claims to Part B. Medicare pays their portion and then forwards the claim to your supplement policy if you have one. The supplement carrier will pay either some or the entire remaining claim depending on the benefits in your policy. If you don't have a supplement policy, the provider bills you for the balance. In contrast, when claims are filed with a Medicare Advantage Plan, the provider files the claim directly with the insurance company running the plan in which you are enrolled. They will pay as your Part A and as your Part B in accordance with the *summary of benefits* or the policy's *evidence of coverage document*.

Pros and Cons

Because choosing the type of Medicare that you take is so important, let's cover some of the pros and cons of each format to give you a feel for both. Your decision will ultimately be affected by several factors, including:

- Your personal health care usage
- Your overall family health care tendencies
- Your current and anticipated overall health status
- Your prescription drug usage
- Your finances
- Your personal health and prescription coverage philosophy

Different underwriting philosophies exist between Medigap policies and Medicare Advantage Plans, however, when you are just starting out with Medicare using your ICEP as a new Medicare enrollee, you are considered *guaranteed issue* with respect to either type of plan. This means that you will not be asked questions about your previous health conditions and you will be covered right away. Like every government program, there are always exceptions. The exception here is that when joining a Medicare Advantage Plan, they can ask you about ESRD. Under certain circumstances, you will still be allowed to join a plan with this condition, but you generally cannot join a Medicare Advantage Plan while suffering from ESRD.

Let's take a look at two scenarios. First, consider a new Medicare enrollee who rarely requires medical services. This individual enjoys very good health and has few major health conditions in his family's history. Let's assume that the only services he uses for the whole first year of his Medicare coverage are five doctor visits—two primary visits and three specialist calls. If this person purchased a supplement policy and a Part D plan, he could easily spend upward of $3,000 on his premium. Five doctor visits at a total cost of $3,000 equates to about $400 per visit—not very economical. In my opinion, any individual using very few services is better off choosing a low premium Medicare Advantage Plan. In so doing, our example patient would pay only a minimal *co-payment* for each visit. Including the premium, he could spend just a few hundred dollars instead of a few thousand dollars in total expenditures for a given year.

The other scenario, of course, is someone who requires many medical services. In this instance, a Medigap policy can be advantageous as essentially two insurances will be paying toward your claims—Original Medicare and the Medigap policy. Depending on the Medigap policy you choose, you may have little or no balance left to pay. Using this plan approach, you pay more up front for premiums but have much lower out-of-pocket expenses for hospital and medical services, supplies, as well as DME used.

High medical usage will work against you in most Medicare Advantage Plans as you must pay the designated cost-sharing amounts until you meet the *out-of-pocket limit*, which is usually in the $3,000 to $8,000 range. As a result, you could end up spending more than you would for a comprehensive Medigap policy. Obviously, no one knows their medical needs in advance. You can, however, look at your tendencies. If you have long-term health conditions that require a lot of care or if you are worried about your future health care needs, you might be better off paying a slightly higher fixed monthly premium for a supplement policy. In so doing, you know that most of your medical expenses will be paid by insurance. Taking this approach allows you to better estimate your monthly and annual costs as there are fewer cost-sharing amounts to consider. Another advantage is that Original Medicare with a Medigap policy allows you to see any doctor and go to any hospital where Original Medicare is accepted. This plan option is free of network and provider restrictions.

So in general terms, Medicare Advantage Plans usually work best for individuals who anticipate low medical service usage. Medicare supplement policies are generally a better fit for individuals who anticipate high medical usage. If you start off with a Medicare Advantage Plan and a new health condition arises, you can always look for a more comprehensive Medicare Advantage Plan the following year—preferably one with lower co-pays for services like hospital stays and medical treatments. The lack of underwriting rules work in your favor. Even if you hit the maximum out-of-pocket cap, you might not spend more than you would have had you bought a supplement policy. This is especially true if you consider the amount of money you would have saved in premium expenses over the years that you maintained the lower cost Medicare Advantage Plan.

There are always opportunities to change from one form of Medicare to another. Each year during the AEP, you may make changes to your Medicare status. In addition, if you join a Medicare Advantage Plan during your ICEP, you can change back to Original Medicare at any point during the first plan year. This is a great way to test-drive a Medicare Advantage Plan to see if it works for you. The only real risk is that if you decide to change to Original Medicare after the first year, you might have to answer medical questions should you choose to get a Medigap policy in the future.

The information presented in the next two chapters is intended to help you decide which form of Medicare will suit you best. Through self-evaluation, you will determine the benefit levels that you need and what features to look for as you consider those plans available to you. Once the self-evaluation process is complete, the form of Medicare that will work best for you should be crystal clear. Once you've made this decision, you can focus in on the plan that best fits your personal health care needs, your lifestyle, and your budget. To be certain that you understand the difference between the two types of Medicare, take a moment to watch this short video on my website: http://medicareplanchoice.com (navigate to "Two ways to get your Medicare video").

The focus of this whole chapter is differentiating between Original Medicare and Part C Medicare Advantage plans. If you are not clear, ask for assistance through the above website or call for telephone support 800-332-7557 8:00 a.m. - 3:00 p.m. EST. every business day.

CHAPTER THREE:

❖

Count Your Health Care Assets and Untangle Your Employer Group Insurance

Now that we've looked at the two distinct forms of Medicare benefits, it's time to take stock of your individual circumstances. The next step in this Medicare decision-making formula is to identify and examine your current health care assets, and see how your existing health care benefits might change as a result of your Medicare eligibility. First, let's look at the health benefits available to you now. These might include an EGHP or benefits through a union, government, or military organization.

One mistake that many new Medicare enrollees make is to jump right in. Many individuals immediately begin comparing plans available through various companies. To immediately begin looking, comparing, and going to seminars and workshops is the wrong approach. First, you must take inventory of your needs, determine what benefits might fit your situation, and examine all of the possibilities that you have already.

I worked with one couple who had taken this hasty approach. They'd begun spinning their wheels, going to meetings, reading manuals, and doing everything they could to look at lots of plans. Finally, someone referred them to me. One of the first questions I asked was whether or not they would have other insurance from an employer, union, or the Department of Veterans Affairs (VA). They indicated that they'd recently retired and had received a benefits package from their former employer. I took a few minutes to examine the company's benefit package and the associated costs. It was clear to me right away that Original Medicare plus the employer-provided coverage would be their best option. They could have avoided a lot of time, effort, and headache by examining what was available to them right from the start.

The most common health care asset held by individuals just becoming eligible for Medicare is an EGHP. This chapter focuses on what to do if you will continue to have a medical plan provided by an employer, union membership, the VA, or another government agency. If these options are not available or if such options will end once you become eligible for Medicare, then skip the rest of this chapter and move on to exploring your health care needs.

Most of the questions asked by new Medicare enrollees surround EGHPs. The use of EGHPs has become more common since full Social Security is offered later than it used to be. If you were born between 1943 and 1954, your full Social Security benefits will be available when you turn sixty-six. For people born after 1954, full Social Security availability is delayed by an additional two months for each year between 1955 and 1959. If you were born in 1960 or beyond, your full Social Security benefits will be available when you turn sixty-seven. Since Medicare benefits currently start at age sixty-five, this leaves many people eligible for Medicare but not yet eligible for their full Social Security benefit for another year or more. Many people therefore continue to work past age sixty-five so that they can collect the full Social Security amount. Because many people already have group insurance through their employer, this raises issues concerning plan coordination. Should you take both parts of Medicare? Should you take just Part A and delay Part B? If you do take Part A or Part B, how will doing so impact your current coverage? In the remainder of this chapter, I'll address the majority of possible scenarios involving group insurance.

Individual with Group Insurance Options

Let's start with a single individual. If you are eligible for Medicare and will either stop working or will continue to work without any form of employer-provided group insurance, you should still consider whether or not you will be eligible for group insurance through a previous employer or military career.

If you are a single individual who plans to continue working until you become eligible for your full Social Security benefits, you must first decide whether or not you will accept Part B. If you meet the eligibility requirements for Part A, then you will take Part A at a minimum as doing so will be free of cost. To determine if accepting Part B is advantageous, examine the plan and the costs associated with the EGHP. Meet with the human resources director at your company to learn about the plans being offered. Ask if the plan benefits and premiums would be different if you were to accept or decline Part B. Some plan benefits differ based on your Medicare eligibility. With this information, you should be able to evaluate the strength of the EGHP with respect to benefits and premiums. Compare the benefits and costs with the Medicare plans available in the public marketplace. Doing so will enable you to select one of three options.

As your first option, you could decline Medicare Part B and keep the EGHP as your primary medical insurance. You would then be able to take Part B later without any penalty as long as you maintain continuous coverage through the EGHP. As your second option, you could accept Part B and keep the EGHP as a supplement policy. Finally, as your third option, you could accept Part B and opt out of the EGHP entirely. You would then choose a Medicare plan from the public marketplace. Just remember that if you compare your EGHP without Part B against public Medicare plans, you must include the additional cost for Part B in your equation.

Couple with EGHP Options

Now let's look at couples. If the older spouse in your household will be eligible for Medicare but will continue to work carrying a nonworking spouse (or working spouse with no other health care options), you may not have many options. In order to take advantage of a public Medicare plan, you would most likely need to disenroll from your EGHP as most group plans include a prescription drug benefit. Medicare does not allow duplication of prescription coverage. You cannot be enrolled in an EGHP that includes a prescription drug component and be enrolled in a Part D plan as well. Under certain circumstances, having a group plan with drug coverage and maintaining a Medigap or medical-only Medicare Advantage Plan makes sense. Most of the time, however, you're stuck carrying the EGHP until the other spouse is eligible for Medicare. Typically, it would be more costly to find medical coverage for the spouse who is not eligible for Medicare outside of the EGHP already in place.

If both you and your spouse are eligible for Medicare and you plan to continue working, you have three basic options. First, you could decline Medicare Part B and keep the EGHP as the primary insurance for one or both of you. Second, you could accept Medicare Part B and keep the EGHP as a supplement policy. This option makes sense if the cost of the EGHP decreases if or when you accept Medicare, thereby offsetting the premium for Part B, and if the EGHP premium is reasonable for both spouses. Lastly, you could accept or decline Part B and keep only the working spouse on the EGHP. The EGHP premium rate is often much lower for just one person versus a couple. You could then shop around for the best individual Medicare plan for the spouse.

In general, I would advise that if you're happy with the EGHP with respect to premiums and benefits, and if the EGHP doesn't mandate that you take your

Part B premium, the EGHP is generally a good alternative. If the EGHP does mandate that you take Part B or if you're not quite satisfied with the plan's premiums or benefits, shop your existing plan against those in the public Medicare marketplace.

If you're looking at plans beyond the EGHP, remember that once you leave the group insurance, you're generally not able to return. You typically cannot go back to the group plan once you disenroll, so make sure that you're leaving for a very good reason. Maybe the premiums are higher than you can afford. Or maybe the premiums are substantially higher than those of plans offering comparable coverage in the open marketplace. Further, the benefits might be less than what you need or they may be substandard compared to the open Medicare plans in relation to the premium cost.

Retaining EGHP Benefits

People who retire from a company but continue to receive medical coverage through that company tend to be very loyal to their former employer. These individuals often accept whatever coverage is offered regardless of the expense. Given recent health care reforms, this approach to choosing coverage can be dangerous. Large companies are experiencing significant impacts as a result of federal mandates. Some insurance rates for employers have increased dramatically. If companies don't differentiate between employees with Medicare and those without, overall insurance rates can be high. Though there is no cut-and-dry formula, it's safe to assume that a retiree paying $250 to $300 per month should shop around to see if a Medicare supplement or Medicare Advantage Plan might be a better approach.

Medicare and EGHP Coordination

If you've made the decision to pair EGHP with Medicare, you should understand how the two policies work together. When you have Medicare in addition to another insurance like an EGHP, certain rules dictate which plan will pay first. The carrier that pays first is called the *primary payer*. The carrier that pays second is called the *secondary payer*. The following chart illustrates how Medicare coordinates with an EGHP.

Medicare / Group insurance coordination chart

Group insurance pays first	Medicare pays first
If you have Medicare because of end-stage renal disease (ESRD): *EGHP* will pay for the first 30 months after you become eligible for Medicare. After 30 months, Medicare pays first.	If you have retiree insurance (insurance from former employment).
If you're 65 or older, have *EGHP* coverage based on your (or your spouse's) current employment, and the employer has 20 or more employees.	If you're 65 or older, have *EGHP* coverage based on your (or your spouse's) current employment, and the employer has less than 20 employees.
If your under 65 and disabled, have *EGHP* coverage based on your (or a family member's) current employment, and the employer has 100 or more employees.	If you're under 65 and disabled, have *EGHP* coverage based on your (or a family member's) current employment, and the employer has less than 100 employees.

Here are some important facts to remember:

- The primary payer pays up to the maximum coverage amount.
- The secondary payer pays only if there are costs not covered by the primary insurer.
- The secondary payer (which may be Medicare) may not pay all of the remaining costs.
- If an EGHP is your secondary payer, you may need to enroll in Medicare Part B before your insurance will pay.
- The following types of insurance typically pay first for particular services:
- No-fault insurance (including automobile insurance)
- Liability (including automobile insurance)
- Black lung benefits
- Workers compensation

Medicaid and TRICARE never pay first for services that are otherwise covered by Medicare. These plans will only pay after Medicare, EGHPs, and/or Medicare supplement insurance plans have paid their portion.

Now that you've examined your health care assets, you may have decided to delay the next step and stay with your EGHP. You may have even discovered an alternative benefit through a previous employer or military career that you'd not previously considered as an option. If that's not the case, then it's time begin looking more closely at your individual health care needs.

EGHP related questions always top the list with new Medicare beneficiaries. Within this subject there are always situations that are neglected to be addressed. If you have a question that has yet to be answered, go to Medicareplanchoice.com and navigate to ask the expert. You can pose your question for a private response. My telephone support line is also available every business day from 8:00 a.m. to 3:00 p.m. EST. at 800-332-7557.

CHAPTER FOUR

Identify the Benefits You Need

During this step, you will identify the types of benefits that you might need. Without this preparation, what would you be looking for? How would you know which plan features are best for you and your situation? Considering your health care needs will enable you to identify exactly what you should be looking for in a plan. Plans that offer lots of features sound great, but if you never use those features then you may be wasting your time and money. My phone has tons of features but if I never use them, how are they beneficial to me? To find the best plan for you, you must know which features are important to you. This requires more self-examination. This preparation is really the hardest part. Consider the work that goes into painting a room. You often spend more time preparing the walls and taping off the surrounding areas, then you actually spend applying the paint. Doing the preparation work now can save you time in the long run by eliminating options that you don't need or want.

Start by asking yourself the health and financial questions included in this chapter. Your answers will help you to identify your individual needs. You can then correlate those needs to the different plan benefit packages and plan formats available in order to find the best fit for your personal situation.

Self-Examination: Health Questions

Ask yourself the following questions related to your health and well-being. Take notes as you go through this section. After each question, I have identified where these items might apply or become a factor as you work to choose the best Medicare plan type for you.

- ✓ What health conditions are you currently receiving treatment for?
- ✓ Do you have any chronic conditions that require continual medical attention, supplies, medical equipment, or other special care?

Supplies and DME fall under Part B and are covered at 80 percent. A Medigap or Medicare supplement policy will generally cover the 20 percent balance after you (or your insurance) pay the deductible for Part B. Most Medicare Advantage Plans, however, will make you pay the 20 percent as a *coinsurance*.

- ✓ How many doctors do you see currently?
- ✓ How would you feel about seeing different doctors?

The number of doctors you see can be a factor in two different ways. First, many of the Medicare Advantage Plans include a fixed co-payment that must be paid at each doctor visit. Visits to see specialists usually include a more expensive co-pay than visits to *primary care physicians* (*PCP*). If you go to the doctor several times each month, these co-pays can add up. Second, many Medicare Advantage Plans have a list of *Participating Providers*. These are doctors who have agreed to accept payments from the Medicare Advantage Plan as part of a contract agreement. The number of eligible doctors who participate in your area may vary. If your doctor does not participate in the plan in which you enroll, you may be forced to change doctors in order to receive plan coverage. As an alternative, you may have to pay a larger share of the medical bill to continue seeing an *out-of-network provider*.

- ✓ Do you primarily travel inside or outside of the United States?

Original Medicare will only pay for coverage in the United States. Some Medicare Advantage and Medigap policies, however, include a foreign travel benefit.

- ✓ Do you have a history of hospital stays?

Hospital stays can be one of the more costly medical services. With either Original Medicare without a Medigap policy or a Medicare Advantage Plan, co-pays for a week or so spent in the hospital can be in the neighborhood of $1,200 to $1,700.

- ✓ Do you have any pending surgeries such as knee or hip procedures?

Surgeries bring hospital costs as well as costs associated with physical therapy. Many patients who undergo knee or hip surgery go to outpatient physical therapy two or three times a week. If you live alone and have no one to assist after this kind of surgery, you might even spend time recuperating in a skilled nursing facility. Such inpatient and outpatient physical therapy visit co-pays can add up.

Self-Examination: Financial Questions

- ✓ How much did you pay for health insurance over the last year?

Consider the amount you'll pay for Medicare Part B. If you subtract this amount from what you paid in health insurance premiums for the last year, you will have an estimated amount to budget for your Medicare health plan. This will keep you close to the amount you spent the previous year.

- ✓ If you were working and paying EGHP premiums will you have the same income when you move to Medicare?

Knowing the impacts of changes to your income will help you make a better plan choice. You don't want to choose a plan and then find that after just a few months, your budget won't cover it. Doing so could force drastic moves that could result in future penalties and even greater expenses.

- ✓ Would you qualify for some of the assistance programs covered in chapter nine of this book?

Some financial assistance programs can lower the costs associated with Medicare Part C and Part D and help to reduce Part B premiums. This could give you some leverage with respect to the monthly premiums associated with your plan.

- ✓ What amount are you comfortable paying for your medical plan?

Knowing your overall budget could very quickly exclude certain plans based strictly on your finances.

Your Personal Philosophy on Health Care

Take some time to consider your personal philosophy regarding health care coverage. Is it important for you to be covered like a blanket, knowing that whatever happens, you will have only a very small financial responsibility? Spending more on monthly premiums might be acceptable if doing so means that you won't experience any big surprises in the form of medical bills. Knowing that they will be living on a fixed income, many people take this stance. A limited monthly allotment does not allow for a lot of medical bill expenditures.

If the questions above related to your prior medical history could be considered nonfactors for you, you can also make a plan choice based solely on the financial aspects. It is important to know the *maximum out-of-pocket expense* amount you are willing to cover. In other words, if you know the absolute most that you can pay for all combined medical expenses in any given year and if you have the necessary finances to cover that amount, then you might consider a plan with more cost sharing and a reasonable cap or limit on total expenses. These plans usually carry lower monthly premium thresholds. Basic Medicare Advantage Plans and high-deductible Medicare supplement policies both offer these types of plans. Choosing one of these plans can ultimately reduce your monthly budget for medical expenses and therefore help to build up your savings. On the other hand, if you don't have the finances available to cover the up-front cost-sharing portions, an affordable plan with a higher premium and lower cost sharing might be a better choice for you.

Consider the following scenario. Let's say you select a Medicare Advantage Plan with drug coverage included that has a maximum out-of-pocket amount of $4,500 for the year. Assume you can get into the plan for a $300 annual premium. You compare that plan against a high-grade Medigap plan that costs $3,000 per year in premiums, taking into consideration the extra cost of a Part D plan. With the Medicare Advantage Plan, you save $2,700 per year in up-front premium costs. Consider this amount to be your gross savings. Your net savings is what remains after you've paid all of the cost-sharing portions that are deemed your responsibility. So if you paid $1,000 in co-payments during the year, you would still be ahead by $1,700. If you required very little health care, this number could be higher. Now consider what would happen if the wheels fell off the cart, so to speak, and you hit your out-of-pocket maximum. Then you would have spent $1,500 more than with the comparable Medigap plan. This type of comparison reveals that by paying the extra premium for the high-grade Medigap policy, you are really spending $3,000 to possibly save $1,500. In my opinion, you're better off saving the money up front and banking the difference. If you make out well for two or three years without any large co-pays, it doesn't matter if you have to pay the maximum; you're already way ahead.

Again, the only real risk here is that if you go beyond the first full year in a Medicare Advantage Plan and you decide to use one of your election periods to go back to Original Medicare and buy a Medigap policy, then you might need to pass some kind of health screening questions to be eligible for the supplement policy. If your overall health falls under certain standards set by the supplement company regarding the health screening questions, you could receive a higher premium rate or even be declined for coverage. If you live in a state where this doesn't apply, however, then you have absolutely nothing to lose. You can pick up a Medigap policy any time in the future with no fear of premium rate increases or preexisting health exclusions.

Answers to these questions will help you to identify whether Original Medicare or Medicare Advantage might work best for you. After analyzing your health care usage, examining the types and amounts of medical services you typically use, and scrutinizing your personal financial philosophy concerning premiums and maximum out-of-pocket expense limits, you should have a good idea as to the best type of Medicare plan for you.

Over the next three chapters, I will focus on the benefits provided by Original Medicare and I will break down Medigap policies, Part D plans, and Medicare Advantage Plans. After considering this information, you should have the necessary background information to select your Medicare plan. If you run into problems, have further questions that are not addressed here, or still feel confused, simply go to http://medicareplanchoice.com and request a personal web chat. I offer my expertise through a personal and private web consultation. There are no fees or obligations. I will provide the answers you need to complete your selection of the right health plan choice. If you need help but don't have access to the Internet, call my toll-free phone line at 800-332-7557 from 8:00 a.m. to 3:00 p.m. EST.

Use this space for notes and calculations:

CHAPTER FIVE:

An Overview of Original Medicare Benefits

Medicare Part A and Part B

Medicare Part A helps to cover the costs associated with inpatient hospital stays, skilled nursing facilities, as well as inpatient mental health, hospice, and home health care. The home care benefit of Medicare covers medically necessary part-time skilled care, which can include physical or speech therapy. A doctor has to order the care and it must be administered by a Medicare-certified home health agency. There is no cost to you for the home health care services covered under original Part A Medicare. To qualify for the hospice benefit, your doctor must certify that you are terminally ill and are expected to live less than six months. Medicare Part A will cover the cost of drugs for pain relief, medical and nursing services, as well as certain medical equipment.

Part A: Cost Sharing for Inpatient Skilled Nursing Stays

Medicare Part A covers short-term stays in confined skilled nursing facilities. It covers room and board (semiprivate), meals, rehabilitative services, and other medically necessary services and supplies. To qualify, you must have been an inpatient in a hospital facility for a minimum of three days. Medicare will cover up to one hundred days in a nursing home, after which you have three choices: pay out of pocket, cash in your long-term care insurance, or apply for Medicaid. Your cost sharing for a Medicare Part A claim associated with a skilled nursing stay is as follows:

- You pay nothing for the first twenty days each *benefit period*. A benefit period is how Medicare measures your use of Skilled Nursing Facility services as well as hospitalization. A benefit period begins the day you're admitted as an inpatient in a hospital or SNF. The benefit period ends

when you haven't received and inpatient care (or skilled care in a SNF) for sixty days in a row.
- You pay a daily coinsurance amount for days twenty-one through one hundred.
- You pay all costs after one hundred days.

Part A: Cost Sharing for Hospitalization

Medicare covers semiprivate rooms, meals, general nursing, and drugs as part of your inpatient care. Medicare does not cover personal care items like razors, slippers, socks, or television and Internet access or telephone use. In addition, you must pay the following for hospital services:

- The Part A deductible ($1,216 for 2014) with no co-payment for days one through sixty each benefit period
- A co-payment for days sixty-one through ninety during each benefit period
- A co-payment for each *lifetime reserve day* used (up to sixty days over your lifetime)
- All costs beyond the lifetime reserve days

The following chart outlines the costs associated with the deductibles, co-payments, and coinsurance for Medicare Part A. The chart includes three columns. The left column is the service type. The middle column identifies what Medicare covers. The right column is the balance left for you to pay. Examining this chart reveals why people who receive benefits through Original Medicare may want to carry additional insurance. A Medicare supplement or Medigap policy can help to cover the balance left behind by Medicare. We will cover this in greater detail when we examine Medigap policies.

An Overview of Original Medicare Benefits

2014 MEDICARE PART A

Part A is Hospital Insurance and covers costs associated with confinement in a hospital or skilled nursing facility.

When you are hospitalized for:	Medicare Covers	You Pay
1 - 60 days	Most confinement costs after the required Inpatient Part A Deductible	$1,216 DEDUCTIBLE
61 - 90 days	All eligible expenses, after the patient pays a $304 per-day copayment	Copay: $304 A DAY as much as $9,120
91 - 150 days (lifetime reserve days)	All eligible expenses, after patient pays a $608 per-day copayment	Copay: $608 A DAY as much as $36,480
151 days or more	NOTHING	YOU PAY ALL COSTS
SKILLED NURSING CARE CONFINEMENT (REHAB)	First 20 days 100% .... Next 80 days You pay $152 per-day	Copay: after 20 days $152 A DAY as much as $12,160

Medicare Part B

Medicare Part B covers outpatient services. This is the broadest category of services encompassing a vast array of items. Most every medical service outside of the hospital is covered under Part B. In general, you pay an annual deductible ($147 for 2014), Medicare pays 80 percent of the approved amount, and you pay the remaining 20 percent. Here are some of the individual items covered under Medicare Part B:

- Ambulance services
- Ambulatory surgical centers
- Cardiac rehabilitation
- Cardiovascular screenings
- Chemotherapy
- Chiropractic services (with some limits on usage)
- Defibrillator implants
- Diabetic supplies
- Doctor and other services
- Durable medical equipment
- Electrocardiogram (EKG)
- Emergency services
- Foot exams and treatment
- Hearing and balance exams (not routine hearing or hearing aids)
- Hepatitis B shots
- HIV screenings
- Home health services
- Kidney dialysis
- Laboratory services
- Mental health care (outpatient)
- Occupational therapy
- Outpatient hospital services
- Outpatient medical and surgical services and supplies
- Physical therapy
- Some prescription drugs (usually administered in a doctor's office)
- Second surgical opinions
- Speech pathology
- Surgical dressing services
- Tests such as X-rays, MRIs, or CAT scans
- Transplants and immunosuppressive drugs
- Urgent care

- Preventive items such as flu shots, mammograms, colorectal screenings, bone mass measurements, pelvic exams, prostate cancer screenings, and HIV screenings

***

Here are a few tips that may be of particular interest to you as the consumer.

- If you want prescription drug coverage while using Original Medicare, you must buy a separate Part D plan. If you delay doing so, you may be charged a penalty.
- Pay attention to the time limits associated with enrollment in Medicare Part B. If you sign up late, you may be penalized.
- Know and understand what costs you would be responsible for when or if you are using straight Medicare with no other insurance to cover your health care. There would be no caps or limits to your liability.
- Your red, white, and blue Medicare card can have your Social Security number imprinted on it. Keep this number safe. Be cautious about showing your card to others. Armed with this sensitive information, identity thieves can build false credit accounts under your name.
- Staying in the hospital overnight does not always mean that you're considered an inpatient. A doctor must admit you in order to be categorized as such. Ask about your status as it can impact what you pay as well as your eligibility for coverage in a skilled nursing facility.

CHAPTER SIX:

❖

Understanding Medicare Supplement Policies

Policies to supplement Original Medicare became available soon after Medicare was initiated. These policies are called Medicare supplement or Medigap policies because they do just that: supplement Medicare and fill in the gaps that Medicare leaves unpaid. In all states except for Massachusetts, Minnesota, and Wisconsin, Medicare supplement policies follow a set of standardized plans. This means that companies are allowed to sell only certain policies. Such standardization is intended to protect consumers.

Prior to standardization, companies would come up with their own list of items that they would agree to cover after Medicare paid. Each company inevitably came up with different benefits, making it was very difficult for consumers to compare plans between companies. After 1992, standardization made it easier for consumers to shop around as all companies offered the same benefits within the designated plan letter. The only remaining variable was the reputation of each insurance company (including financial rating, strength, size, and so forth), the premium amount charged for the designated policy, and the customer service level of that company or the company's representative or agent.

Policies that were sold prior to standardization are still active and may contain some benefits that the newer, standardized plans do not. Companies were no longer able to sell these plans; therefore, they were not able to spread their risk. As people dropped the plans or died off, the policies became more and more expensive. Undoubtedly, some still remain. The newer, standardized policies have been designated by letters (A, B, C, and so forth) and have undergone revision multiple times. Even some of the standardized policies are now considered extinct and are no longer sold. These include plans E, H, I, and J. The current designated plan letters are A, B, C, D, F, F*, G, K, L, M, and N. Take a few minutes to watch a short video on Medicare supplement policies on my website: http://medicareplanchoice.com. The following illustration provides a list of the current Medicare supplement policies.

10 STANDARD MEDICARE SUPPLEMENT PLANS

A	B	C	D	F	G	K	L	M	N
BASIC BENEFITS	BASIC BENEFITS	BASIC BENEFITS	BASIC BENEFITS	BASIC BENEFITS	BASIC BENEFITS	BASIC BENEFITS*	BASIC BENEFITS*	BASIC BENEFITS*	BASIC BENEFITS*
	PART A DEDUCTIBLE	PART A DEDUCTIBLE	PART A DEDUCTIBLE	PART A DEDUCTIBLE	PART A DEDUCTIBLE	PART A DEDUCTIBLE*	PART A DEDUCTIBLE*	PART A DEDUCTIBLE*	PART A DEDUCTIBLE
		SKILLED NURSING CO-INSURANCE	SKILLED NURSING CO-INSURANCE	SKILLED NURSING CO-INSURANCE	SKILLED NURSING CO-INSURANCE	SKILLED NURSING CO-INSURANCE*	SKILLED NURSING CO-INSURANCE*	SKILLED NURSING CO-INSURANCE*	SKILLED NURSING CO-INSURANCE
		PART B DEDUCTIBLE		PART B DEDUCTIBLE					
				PART B EXCESS CHARGES	PART B EXCESS CHARGES				
		FOREIGN TRAVEL	FOREIGN TRAVEL	FOREIGN TRAVEL	FOREIGN TRAVEL			FOREIGN TRAVEL	FOREIGN TRAVEL
						OUT OF POCKET MAX $4,260	OUT OF POCKET MAX $2,310		

- In the table above, you can see all plans include the basic benefits. Basic benefits consist of three items. Fist, the extended hospitalization days (the days after one through 60). The second item is the first three pints of blood that are administered during a treatment. And lastly, the 20 percent (of the approved amount) balance of Part B expenses left after Medicare pays their 80 percent (of the approved amount). The following plans deviate from these basic benefit coverage rules and are designated with an asterisk:
- Plan K pays 10 percent(of the approved amount)
- Plan L pays 15 percent(of the approved amount)
- Plan N includes a co-pay of up to $20 per doctor visit and a $50 co-pay for an emergency room visit that does not result in an admission

The Part A deductible benefit pays the full deductible with these exceptions:
- Plan K pays 50 percent of the Part A deductible
- Plan L pays 75 percent of the Part A deductible
- Plan M pays 50 percent of the Part A deductible

Finally, the skilled nursing coinsurance benefit pays the co-insurance balance for days twenty one through one hundred with these exceptions:
- Plan K pays 50 percent of the co-insurance
- Plan L pays 75 percent of the co-insurance

High deductible plan F
- Plan F* is available as a standard plan or a high deductible plan

The chart of the ten standard Medicare supplement plans lists each plan as well as the items covered under each plan. Plan A provides the least coverage and includes just the basic benefits. Plan F is considered the most comprehensive, covering both Part A and Part B deductibles as well as a skilled nursing benefit, foreign travel, and excess charges. As the chart shows, all of the policies include the *basic benefits* (some being modified as noted). As an agent, I have always referred to coverage of three particular items as *core benefits*. These benefits provide a high threshold of coverage for the insured. The core benefits include the basic benefits, the Part A deductible, and the skilled nursing benefit. The basic benefits protect some very large extended hospital stay co-pays as well as the 20 percent left on Part B expenses. The Part A deductible benefit will cover up to five admissions per year. This could cost more than $5,000. Finally, the skilled nursing benefit provides coinsurance in case you go beyond twenty days in a nursing home. Medicare would leave a balance of $152 a day. After eighty days, that would result in a bill for $12,160. Just these three benefits could save you more than $50,000 in bills. The plans that offer these core benefits include C, D, F, G, and N.

The following chart shows these core benefits along with "gaps" they fill using the overview of part A from the last chapter. This time the Medicare supplement benefits are shown on the right correlating to the items they would cover.

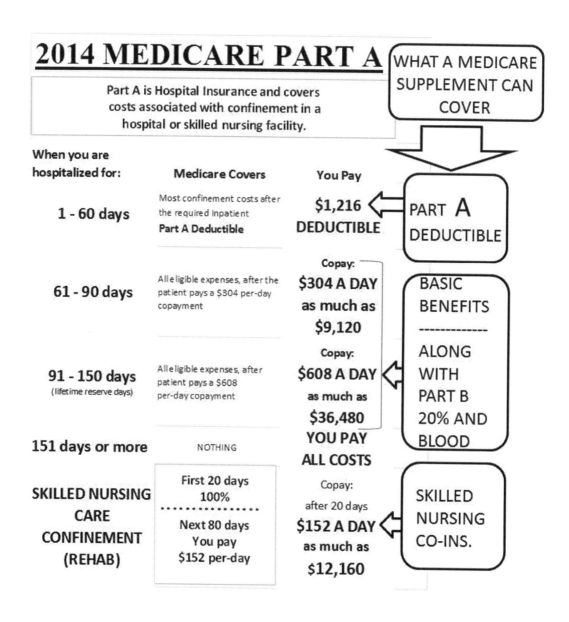

Understanding Medicare Supplement Policies

In my opinion, the annual Part B deductible is not critical as it reflects a finite amount, which is currently under $150 for an entire year. As for the excess charge benefit, in most states laws govern how much providers are legally able to charge above the Medicare allowable amount. Therefore, I don't consider this benefit to be critical. It may become critical in the future, however, given the swift changes in health care laws and the proposed cuts currently being made in Medicare spending. Many physicians are being squeezed so hard by the reduction of Medicare reimbursements that they may begin adding excess charges to their bill. Until I see this happen on a consistent basis, however, I would not consider the excess charge benefit a must-have. With respect to the foreign travel benefit, you must decide how important that would be for you. Medicare only provides coverage within the United States. If you travel frequently, you might consider the foreign travel benefit advantageous. Travel insurance, by contrast, provides a little more flexibility. You can purchase this coverage when you travel rather than paying for it as a fixed benefit every month as part of your health policy package.

Plans K, L, and M all include larger out-of-pocket expenses. To offset this, they each apply a maximum out-of-pocket limit. If you hit the limit, the insurance plan will cover the remainder of your bills for the rest of the benefit year providing they are plan covered expenses. As an incentive to enroll, these policies offer lower monthly premiums.

As an agent, I recommend Plan F if you use lots of medical services such as hospital stays, multiple doctor visits, medical equipment including oxygen, or ongoing tests and treatments. Although the premium is higher, Plan F currently covers everything that Medicare leaves behind. This would be the best choice for someone who wants to feel "covered like a blanket" with no expectations for out-of-pocket expenses.

If you don't mind paying some bills but want full coverage for the big items, I recommend Plan N. It provides full hospital coverage, skilled nursing coinsurance, and 20 percent of medical expenses. The only items that you pay for include the annual Part B deductible (which is currently $147), a $20 co-pay for doctor visits (primary or specialist), and a $50 co-pay in the emergency room if you are not admitted. Though you will pay some smaller bills, you'll save a lot on premium payments in comparison with Plan F. Consider the example shown below. This person used a hospital stay, a skilled nursing facility for twenty-three days, and a couple of doctor visits. The chart compares the use of these services across Plan F, Plan N, and straight Medicare. The dollar amounts shown reflect the out-of-pocket costs that the insured would be required to pay. Notice how the insured would pay a relatively small amount under Plan N as compared to straight Medicare.

Expense comparison between Original Medicare and plans N, and F

SERVICE TYPE	ORIGINAL MEDICARE ONLY	MEDICARE SUPPLEMENT PLAN N	MEDICARE SUPPLEMENT PLAN F
Part A deductible for Hospital stay	$1216	0	0
Skilled nursing facility stay Days 21-23 ($152 X 3)	$456	0	0
Part B deductible for the year	$147	$147	0
Part B co-insurance 2 visits	$40	$40	0
Total for a hospital stay, 23 days in skilled nursing and 2 doctor visits	$1859	$187	0

Rating and Underwriting

Medicare supplement policies are underwritten according to three different philosophies. Each uses a distinct factor to calculate premiums. Differences also exist among the underwriting process or procedure that each company uses to gauge assumed risk by issuing a policy. Each form of underwriting offers pros and cons. Some states allow all three to be used, though one form typically dominates the marketplace in each state.

The first type of underwriting is referred to as *community rated*. This means that the premiums are calculated by geographical area using zip codes. Premiums are higher or lower depending on where you live. As an example, I live in New York. The counties upstate have lower premium rates than the counties in the metropolitan New York City area. Premiums cannot be increased as a result of age or medical use; however, companies can increase premiums to adjust for inflation and other factors. There is also no medical underwriting in the state of New York. This means that if you have Part A and Part B of Medicare and you have the money to pay the first month's premium, you must be issued a policy regardless of your current or past health conditions. In New York state insurance companies can apply a six-month preexisting condition exclusion unless the issue of the policy was during a guaranteed-issue timeframe. In other words the issuing insurance company may not cover any preexisting health condition until you have been on the new policy for six months. This can occur if you did not have either another Medicare supplement policy or a Medicare Advantage Plan in place within sixty-three days of applying for the policy.

The second type of underwriting is referred to as *issue age* or *entry age*. In this scenario, premium amounts are determined according to what age you were when you bought the policy (or the time of policy issue). As with community-rated policies, the premiums can be increased to account for inflation and other factors. They cannot, however, be increased due to your age.

The last type of underwriting is called *attained age*. Premiums for this type of policy are based on your current age. These are often the least expensive initially, though they can eventually become the most expensive as the premiums can be increased to account for inflation and other factors as well as your age.

All Medicare supplement policies are issues as guaranteed renewable. As a result, companies cannot cancel your policy due to high medical usage.

Guaranteed-Issue Timing for Medicare Supplement

Under certain circumstances, insurance companies are required to sell you a Medigap policy. In accordance with your guaranteed-issue rights, companies cannot refuse you, though they may be able to limit your choice of policies. These circumstances, which extend beyond your initial enrollment period, include the following:

- If you are enrolled in a Medicare Advantage Plan and that plan ends in your area or if you move out of that plan's service area
- If you are covered through an employer or a union and that coverage ends
- If you have original Medicare and are enrolled in a Medicare SELECT plan (a Medigap policy wherein you agree to see certain doctors and hospitals) and you move outside of the applicable service area
- If you joined a Medicare Advantage Plan when you were first eligible at sixty-five and within the first year of joining, you decide to switch back to Original Medicare
- If you dropped a Medigap policy to join a Medicare Advantage Plan for the first time and, after being in that plan less than a year, you decide to switch back
- If your Medigap insurance company goes bankrupt or your Medigap policy ends through no fault of your own

- If you drop a Medigap policy or leave a Medicare Advantage Plan because the company didn't follow the rules or misled you

If you find yourself in any of these circumstances, you don't have to worry about answering any medical questions when picking up a Medigap policy even if the company you are applying with normally would ask them. If you simply wish to change from one Medigap company to another, you can do so at any point during the year. There are no election periods that regulate when you can make changes. Depending on the method of underwriting used by the Medigap policy, you might need to go through an underwriting process during which you will be asked about your medical history. Depending on the company's guidelines, they may be able to refuse coverage or make you pay increased premium amounts if you experienced certain health problems or took certain prescription drugs.

Defy the Laws of Insurance

If you live in a state that issues community-rated plans with no medical underwriting, you won't have to answer any medical questions. In this case, you can shop strictly based on price. There are no time limits and no underwriting restrictions to hold you back. This gives you what I consider to be the ultimate consumer advantage. If you're in good health and you use minimal services, you can enroll in a Medicare Advantage Plan wherein you will pay low premium amounts and minimal co-pays. If you begin to use more services or develop a long-term chronic health condition that demands more care, you can use your annual election period or an SEP if you're eligible to return to Original Medicare and purchase a Medigap policy. Doing so will cover all of these ailments with no health questions or preexisting condition limitations.

Under these circumstances, one could claim that you're actually defying the rules of insurance. Think about a homeowner's insurance policy. Could you wait until your house caught on fire to buy a policy covering fire damage? There's no chance. This anomaly in health coverage is currently viable. Using an insurance agent like me provides the same benefits of hiring an accountant or a lawyer. We know and understand the intricacies of such anomalies, details that could save you thousands of dollars. Best of all, insurance agents are paid by the insurance companies. This means that we're essentially working for you for free. Again, if you'd like to discuss your individual circumstances, or just want a quote on a Medicare supplement policy, you can request a web chat through my website http://medicareplanchoice.com. I can give you a quote on a

Medigap policy or arrange a meeting to consider your circumstances and to address any questions you may have free of obligations or fees.

***

Here are a few tips concerning Medicare supplements that may be of particular interest to you as the consumer.

- You are guaranteed issue of a Medicare supplement when first taking your Medicare Part B even if you delayed doing so as long as you had continual coverage from an employer or spousal employer. Regardless of your current health, all of your conditions will be covered.
- Medicare supplement policies are standardized everywhere except for Massachusetts, Minnesota, and Wisconsin. This means that regardless of which letter plan you're considering, coverage will be identical with every company. As long as you are happy with a particular company with respect to their service and rating, choose the company with the lowest premium.
- Don't forget that if you buy a Medigap policy to supplement Original Medicare and you want prescription drug coverage so that you will not be penalized later, you must also purchase a Part D drug plan. Medicare and Medigap policies do not cover prescription drugs.
- You can change your Medicare supplement policy at any time during the year. There is no election period.
- Don't try to compare a Medicare supplement policy to a Medicare Advantage Plan. Make sure that you thoroughly understand what form of Medicare coverage you are comparing.

CHAPTER SEVEN:

❖

Understanding Medicare Advantage Plans

As part of the Balanced Budget Act of 1997, Medicare was allowed to subcontract private companies to perform administration. Though it took the companies a few years to develop and release the Medicare Advantage Plans, about 25 percent of the Medicare population is now enrolled in this form of Medicare.

If you enroll in a Medicare Advantage Plan, you still have Medicare coverage and are entitled to all Part A and Part B benefits. Private insurance companies simply do all of the administration and pay all of the claims. Medicare pays these companies subsidy dollars from the money you pay for Medicare Part B premiums. The amount that the insurance companies receive differs from county to county based on a complex formula. This formula takes into consideration 122 demographic factors including population, age, gender, and health claims. Medicare Advantage Plans must spend a certain portion of the money that they receive on consumer benefits. As a result, many of the plans include Part D drug benefits with the Part A and Part B benefits. In some instances, these plans also provide benefits that go beyond what Original Medicare covers. They may also provide benefits such as gym memberships, prescription glasses, and routine dental coverage. Because they are subsidized by Medicare, Medicare Advantage Plans offer low monthly premiums. In fact, some plans in certain areas of the country have a zero monthly premium. It's easy to see why they've become popular.

Medicare Advantage Plans operate in several different formats. The most common are as follows: *HMO (Health Maintenance Organization)*, *PPO (Preferred Provider Organization)*, *PFFS (Private Fee-for-Service)*, *SNP (Special Needs Plan)*, and *MSA (Medical Savings Account)*. We'll discuss each form in detail here, but I recommend taking a few minutes to watch a short video on this subject at the following website: http://medicareplanchoice.com

Health Maintenance Organization (HMO)

Let's start with the HMO. This form of Medicare Advantage incorporates a list of contracted doctors and hospitals. These providers have agreed to certain terms and conditions of payment associated with the HMO plan. Under this form of coverage, you can use only those providers within the network. Except for an emergency service, if you use a provider outside of the plan, you may become responsible for the total expense. Some HMO plans do include a *point-of-service* (*POS*) option, which allows receipt of certain services out of network. Otherwise, you must remain in network. Overall, HMOs are considered the most restrictive plan format with rules that can include preauthorization for certain diagnostic tests or a written referral from your *PCP* should you wish to see a specialist. On the other hand, if all of the doctors that you see are in the network anyway, or if you are willing to be flexible with respect to the doctors you visit, HMOs sometimes provide extra perks such as gym memberships, preventive care, and comprehensive dental services. Lastly, most HMO plans include the Part D drug benefit as part of the overarching plan. As such, one card can be used for all Medicare-covered services including doctor visits, hospital visits, and prescription drugs.

Preferred Provider Organization (PPO)

PPOs are similar to HMOs in that they also contract with particular physicians and hospitals, encouraging plan members to visit these preferred providers. If you go outside of the network, you will still be covered as long as the provider you seek is willing to bill your PPO plan as an out-of-network provider. You will typically pay a little more for out-of-network services, but having this ability can give members peace of mind if they must seek services far from home. Again, emergency services are covered anywhere in the United States and are treated as in-network services in accordance with federal law. PPOs also tend to include the Part D drug benefit, though if you already receive drug coverage from the VA or through an EGHP, some PPOs offer plans for doctor and hospital coverage only.

Private Fee-for-Service (PFFS)

A PFFS plan is similar to Original Medicare which is considered to be a fee for service insurance. You can generally go to any doctor or hospital that will accept the plan's terms and conditions. Under a PFFS plan, providers do not need to be under contract. In other words, they do not have a predetermined fee schedule for payment by the insurance company. Instead, these providers essentially piggyback the Medicare contract already in place. As a result,

PFFS plan reimbursement rates usually mirror those of Original Medicare. Whatever a hospital or doctor could expect to be paid by Medicare is also what they can expect from the PFFS Medicare Advantage Plan. Given these factors, I believe that PFFS plans are the least restrictive type of Medicare Advantage Plan. I frequently recommend this type to my clients. Many PFFS plans include a Part D drug benefit; however, if that component is not built into the plan benefits you always have the option to carry a separate Part D plan for drug coverage.

Special Needs Plan (SNP)

An SNP includes certain criteria that must be met prior to enrollment. Unlike standard Medicare Advantage Plans that use specific enrollment periods, SNPs allow you to enroll at any time during the year provided you meet the enrollment criteria. Though there are several different enrollment qualifiers in the marketplace, I will identify three here.

The first type of SNP is for individuals who receive state medical assistance also known as *Medicaid*. If a person is eligible for both Medicare and Medicaid, that person would be referred to as *dual eligible*. With most plans, it's usually necessary to verify one's eligibility for Medicaid in order to join. If you can qualify for this type of plan, the extra benefits that most companies offer tend to be very good. Dual-eligible individuals are highly sought after by Medicare Advantage Plans as the insurance companies can receive higher subsidy levels when these individuals are enrolled in their plans.

Another qualifier for an SNP is diagnosis with certain chronic health conditions such as heart disease, chronic obstructive pulmonary disease, or diabetes. Again, this qualification would need to be verified by your family doctor or the specialist who rendered the initial diagnosis. These plans usually offer benefits associated with these conditions, such as therapy at a reduced cost, diabetic supplies, and expanded drug formularies including both brand-name and generic drugs used to treat particular conditions.

A third qualifier for an SNP is institutionalization, typically in a long-term nursing home. These plans sometimes mirror the Original Medicare co-pay and coinsurance schedule, though they also include some of the extra benefits mentioned previously. One common benefit is coverage of over-the-counter products. This can be very useful as many patients in nursing homes are on full Medicaid for payment, which can limit their spendable income for products like toothpaste, hair products, and vitamins to as little as $50 per month.

Medical Savings Account (MSA)

MSAs essentially combine a high-deductible health plan with a bank account. Medicare deposits money into the account (usually less than the deductible), which can then be used to pay for health care services throughout the year.

How the Medicare Advantage Plans Work

Now that we've looked at the types of Medicare Advantage Plans, let's examine how they work. As mentioned previously, Medicare compensates these companies for their administration of Part A, Part B, and Part D benefits. The Medicare Advantage Plans might also charge you a premium to be a member. As a member, you will receive a summary of benefits and a document providing evidence of coverage. This is essentially your insurance policy. It spells out exactly what the plan will cover and what you are responsible for. The amounts for which you are responsible are usually considered co-payments and coinsurances. Co-payments represent a fixed amount paid for a specific service. For example, the plan may specify a $15 co-payment for a PCP visit. This means that regardless of what the doctor charges and regardless of what the insurance actually pays the doctor, you will be responsible for just $15. Coinsurance, in contrast, is calculated as a percentage of the total bill. For instance, if your plan specified a 20 percent coinsurance payment for a piece of DME like a walker or wheelchair, you must pay 20 percent of the approved amount. The approved amount is equal to the agreed-upon price for said product or service as determined by the provider during contract negotiations. Medicare is often used as a benchmark for payment amounts. Providers can therefore expect an amount similar to what Original Medicare might approve. The approved amount term is similar to the *usual and customary* language found in traditional health insurance policies.

Medicare Advantage Plans are similar to an à la carte menu. You pay for services as you use them. If you use very few services and your plan premium is low, then you will pay little for coverage. However, if you use a lot of expensive services such as hospital stays, extended skilled nursing stays, treatment for cancer or other diseases, you will be responsible for the co-payments and coinsurances until you reach the maximum annual out-of-pocket amount. That amount can range from $3,000 to $10,000. If you reach that amount, the plan will pay 100 percent of the remaining bills for the rest of that benefit year, provided they fall within the plan's covered services.

Once you've enrolled in a Medicare Advantage Plan, you're usually expected to remain in that plan for the entire year or until the next AEP (unless you qualify for an SEP). If you join a Medicare Advantage Plan when you are first eligible for Medicare benefits, you have the right to change back to Original Medicare at any point during that first year. This is a great way to test-drive a Medicare Advantage Plan when you first enroll in Medicare. If you decide that you don't like it, you can simply opt to go back to Original Medicare and then add a Part D plan as well as a Medigap policy if you prefer.

To find a Medicare Advantage plan in your area, go to http://medicare-planchoice.com and click on get a quote or web chat, or call 800-332-7557 every business day between 8 am. and 3 pm. EST.

***

Here are a few tips concerning Medicare Advantage Plans that may be of particular interest to you as the consumer.

- Because all Medicare Advantage Plans incorporate different levels of out-of-pocket expenses, be sure to compare the outline of benefits for each company under consideration. Most companies use the same general categories, which enables you to compare each category to determine which company offers the best coverage levels for the services you use.
- Make sure that you understand which format your Medicare Advantage Plan follows. You don't want to be surprised in the future by a preauthorization requirement for diagnostic tests or the need to obtain referrals to see specialists.
- Don't forget that you have the right to change from a Medicare Advantage Plan back to Original Medicare at any time during the first year of coverage as well as on an annual basis during the AEP, the MADP, or at any point with an SEP.
- Choose a plan that suits your current level of medical service usage. If your health changes, you can always switch to a different Medicare Advantage Plan the next year with no medical questions.
- Don't get confused and compare Medicare Advantage Plans to Medicare supplement policies. Be sure that you thoroughly understand the form of Medicare coverage that you're comparing.
- If you choose a Medicare Advantage Plan, be sure to understand whether or not it includes a Part D component. Some Medicare Advantage Plans are sold without drug coverage. Avoid being penalized in the future for going without such coverage.

- Make sure to read your *annual notice of change (ANOC)*. This document identifies what changes will occur within the policy in the upcoming year. This may include premium, co-pay, or coinsurance changes, as well as drug formulary changes.

CHAPTER EIGHT:

❖

Understanding Medicare Part D and the Doughnut Hole

To round out your Medicare coverage, let's take a look at Part D. Established in 2006, Part D is the primary means by which Medicare enrollees receive coverage for prescription drugs. Like Medicare Advantage, all of the Part D plans are administered by private insurance companies. There are two ways to get part D. First, if you are enrolled in Original Medicare, you have what is referred to as a stand-alone Part D or prescription drug plan (PDP). If you are enrolled in a Medicare Advantage Plan that contains a Part D component, you are enrolled in a Medicare Advantage Prescription Drug or MAPD plan.

Prior to 2006, it was very difficult to find any drug coverage at all. People used discount cards or even traveled to drugstores in Canada in order to fill their more expensive prescriptions. Although the current system still contains the dreaded *doughnut hole* or coverage gap, people with extreme drug needs can still save a lot of money. Once a patient reaches what is referred to as *catastrophic coverage*, the drug costs are very low. The coverage gap is scheduled to be eliminated in 2020 as part of the Patient Protection and Affordable Care Act. For an overview of Part D, please refer to the related video posted as follows: http://medicareplanchoice.com.

The Four Stages of Part D

First, let's consider the technical aspects of Part D. All Part D plans follow the same fundamental framework. This framework consists of four stages of coverage. The first stage is the deductible, which is the amount that the patient must pay before the plan will begin to pay. Though not all plans include a deductible, for those that do, the standard deductible for 2014 is $310.

Next is the initial coverage stage. During this phase of coverage, when you fill prescriptions, you pay one amount and the insurance pays another amount toward the total cost of the drug. Some plans use a co-pay at this stage while others use a coinsurance amount. This stage continues until the total cost—what you pay plus what your insurance pays—reaches the coverage limit ($2,850 for 2014).

At this point, you've reached the dreaded doughnut hole. This term simply means that you have exhausted the initial coverage limit of the policy. For drugs purchased during this stage, you pay a percentage of the manufacturer's discounted price. The government covers a portion of the cost as well. In 2014, plan members pay 47.5 percent for brand-name drugs and 72 percent for generic drugs. This stage continues until you reach your annual out-of-pocket amount for drug costs ($4,550 in 2014).

This marks the final stage, the catastrophic stage, wherein the insurance policy begins to cover drug costs. At this point, you pay the greater between 5 percent coinsurance and $2.55 co-pay for generic or $6.35 co-pay for brand-name drugs.

Part D Formulary

Now that we've looked at the technical aspects of Part D, let's concentrate on the surrounding parts. Whether you get a Part D stand-alone or through a Medicare Advantage Plan, the plans follow the same stages. The plans differ because each has a unique *formulary* or list of drugs covered by that particular plan. Checking the plan's formulary is the only way to tell if the medications that you take will be covered. To do so, you must take the time to research whether or not your prescriptions are referenced in the plan materials provided. Most plans include many common drugs that are prescribed regularly, so if you take just a few common drugs, you have the broadest range of plans available to consider. If, however, your list of prescribed medications is long and contains a lot of brand-name drugs, the plan choices you have may be considerably fewer. Your philosophy regarding brand-name medications versus generic medications will ultimately determine which plans will fit you best. Generic drug manufacturers will tell you that the generic form contains the same active ingredients as the brand-name drug. But some people can't tolerate various ingredients in the generic form, so they stay with the brand-name drugs. If you're willing to take the generic form as opposed to the brand-name form, you'll have an easier time finding a drug plan that fits your needs.

Drug Tiers

Whether included in a Part C plan or as a stand-alone PDP, most Part D plans separate the drugs that they cover into *drug tiers* or categories. Some plans use a four-tier system while others use a five-tier system. Under a four-tier system, the categories are as follows: generic, brand name, nonpreferred brand name, and specialty. A five-tier system uses the following tiers: preferred generic, non-preferred generic, preferred brand name, nonpreferred brand name, and specialty. Your cost-sharing amount increases as the tier numbers increase. So tier one reflects the lowest cost and tier five reflects the highest cost. You can lower your personal drug expenses by using prescriptions in the lowest possible category. Pharmacies automatically substitute a brand-name drug with the generic form if a generic is available. The one exception is if your doctor writes *DAW* or *dispense as written* on the prescription. In this case, you must speak with your doctor to make any adjustments to the prescriptions dispensed.

Formulary Restrictions

When you are researching a drug plan's formulary, it's important to pay attention to the three different designations that appear in the formulary directories. If you find your drug listed in the formulary but one of these designations is attached, then the plan will cover the drug but will impose other requirements or limits. For instance, if your drug is designated *prior authorization*, then the plan requires that you or your physician get authorization from the plan prior to filling the prescription. More often than not, your doctor will work with the plan to do so. Your drug might be designated as *quantity limits* in which case only a limited quantity of the drug can be dispensed. As an example, the plan may limit patients to sixty tablets a month for a certain drug. If your prescription is written for a higher quantity, you will need authorization from your doctor before the plan will fill the full prescription. Lastly, the designation *step therapy* requires that you try to treat your condition using other drugs before the plan will authorize that particular drug. Your doctor can verify whether or not you have already tried the alternatives.

Formulary Exceptions

Plans may consider adding your particular drug or drugs into their formulary if those drugs are currently excluded. To do so will involve requesting a *formulary exception*. During this process, your doctor and the plan will exchange correspondence. If you've tried all of the alternatives, or if your doctor insists that you take a certain drug, adjustments can be made by the plan through an *appeals process*. Depending on your prescription requirements, this aspect of a Part D plan can be very important as you pursue your decision-making process.

Medicare Part D plan premiums are usually lower when they are included in a Medicare Advantage Plan. Because these companies are already being compensated for administering health benefits, they can give their members a lower rate for the drug plan. The stand-alone Part D drug plans range from $15 a month to well over $100, though most are around $50 a month. A complete list of the drug plans in your area is available through the plan-finding tool on Medicare's website. Like Medicare Advantage Plans, you can change your Part D plan every year during the AEP or at any time if you qualify for a SEP.

Income Related Monthly Adjustment Amount

Similar to how your Medicare Part B premium can be affected by the income amount reported to Social Security, your Part D premium can be affected with an *Income Related Monthly Adjustment Amount or IRMAA*. If the income reported over the prior two years exceeds certain thresholds, you will pay an added amount on top of the standard premium amount advertised by all Part D plans. Here is a chart showing the income levels and the adjustment amounts that could be added to your Part D premium.

Income Related Monthly Adjustment Amount

If Your Yearly Income in 2012 Was			You Pay in 2014
File Individual Tax Return	File Joint Tax Return	File Married & Separate Return	
Under $85,000	Under $170,000	Under $85,000	Your Plan Premium
$85,001 to $107,000	$170,001 to $214,000	N/A	$12.10 Plus Your Plan Premium
$107,001 to $160,000	$214,001 to $320,000	N/A	$31.10 Plus Your Plan Premium
$160,001 to $214,000	$320,001 to $428,000	$85,000 to $129,000	$50.20 Plus Your Plan Premium
$214,001+	$428,001+	$129,001+	$69.30 Plus your Plan Premium

Part D LEPs and Creditable Coverage

If you don't enroll in a Medicare Part D plan when you first become eligible, you may have to pay penalties in the future unless you had another prescription plan that was considered *creditable coverage*. This means that the prescription

==coverage was at least equal to or greater than the benchmark Part D plan.== Such penalties are not one-time fines. Once assessed, the LEP's continue as long as you are in a Part D plan. Because the penalty amounts are based on the average cost of a Part D plan across the country and those costs continue to increase, the penalties can be stiff. The current penalty is 1 percent per month for the number of months you did not have coverage. So let's say you were eligible for Part D. Because you didn't have any prescriptions, you decided not to enroll in a plan right away. Four years later, you have a serious health situation. Your doctor tells you that without a certain drug, your life span will decrease drastically. Now you need a Part D plan, but you might have to wait until the AEP to be eligible to join. While you wait for the AEP, you must pay full price for the drugs out of pocket. Eventually, you join a plan with a $50 monthly premium. Here's how the penalty is assessed: forty-eight months without coverage equates to a 48 percent penalty. Let's say that the average plan is also $50. As a result, $24 (or 48 percent of $50) is added to your premium making it $74. Though it's true that you would have spent a lot of money on premiums for a Part D plan that you didn't initially need, the penalty amounts associated with picking up the Part D plan later will continue to rise. If the price of the average plan goes to $100, then you would pay $48 in penalty charges on top of the $100 premium. If you're just joining Medicare and don't currently take any drugs, you may be tempted not to take a drug plan in order to avoid paying for a plan that you wouldn't use. In my opinion, you're better off finding the drug plan with the lowest premium available—whether it's a stand-alone PDP or an MAPD—and paying the premium just to avoid future penalties. Again, because the penalties are based on future averages, they are greatly affected by inflation. The bottom line is that you want to avoid penalties. If penalties are assessed and you believe that they are incorrect, you can file an appeal at the following site: http://www.medicarepartdappeals.com/. Penalties can also be eliminated if you qualify for extra help with Part D. To apply, go to http://www.socialsecurity.gov/prescriptionhelp/. The next chapter includes further details.

***

Here are a few tips concerning Medicare Part D that may be of particular interest to you as the consumer.

- Be sure to check the plan's formulary prior to enrollment to be sure that the drugs you take will be covered and to determine whether or not they carry restrictions.

- Decide on a plan based on expectations of premium level, deductible, and cost sharing for the drugs that you currently take.
- Be sure to take advantage of any state or federal assistance for which you might qualify. This will be discussed further in the next chapter.
- Know if you qualify for any SEPs.
- Make sure to read the ANOC, which outlines any policy changes that will occur in the upcoming year. This might include premium, co-pay, or coinsurance changes, as well as drug formulary changes.

CHAPTER NINE:

❖

Getting Extra Help from Federal, State, and Local Sources

One of the first things that I do when meeting with a Medicare-eligible individual is to try and help them find as many sources of assistance as I can. There are often ways to leverage that assistance in order to receive the maximum benefit. This chapter describes where to look for help and how to apply. Most programs are income and resource sensitive; to apply you must meet certain criteria. I will identify the major programs that I consider and where to find them.

First, let's look at the federal government. These programs will give you the largest benefit, but they are also the hardest to qualify for. The Medicare savings program, though a federal program, is administered by the state through each county's social services department. If you qualify for this program, Uncle Sam will pay for your Part B premium each month you're eligible. Because Part B premiums are over $100 a month now, this can save you more than $1,200 per year with money added directly to your Social Security check. The qualifications change annually and each state may calculate your income differently.

There are four kinds of Medicare savings programs. The *Qualified Medicare Beneficiary (QMB) Program* helps to pay for Part A and/or Part B premiums, deductibles, coinsurances, and co-payments. An individual in the *Specified Low-Income Medicare Beneficiary (SLMB) Program* receives help with the Part B premium only. An individual in the *Qualifying Individual (QI) Program* also receives help with Part B premiums, however, participants must apply each year and spots are granted on a first-come, first-served basis. Finally, a participant in the *Qualified Disabled and Working Individuals (QDWI) Program* receives help with Part A premiums only as participants must be working with certain disabilities to qualify. For most of these programs, the income qualification for a single person needs to be less than $1,313 per month. Resources limits are also imposed. Resources counted include amounts in savings, checking, retirement accounts, as well as stocks and bonds, your home and vehicle are not counted however a vacation home would be. Resources must be less than $7,080 for qualification as an individual. As a married couple, the current limits are $1,765 for income and $10,620 for resources. Again, these numbers change annually. Because some states calculate income differently, it's worth applying if you think you might be close to these numbers. To apply, visit your local social services office

The Extra Help program through Social Security provides assistance with premiums, deductibles, coinsurances, and co-payments associated with Part D. If you qualify, you will also be exempt from the coverage gap or doughnut hole associated with Part D and any late enrollment penalties will be wiped out. Again, the numbers change annually. In 2014, you can qualify as a single with income under $17,235 and resources under $13,300. As a couple, the current limit is $23,265 for income and $26,580 for resources. Apply online as follows: http://www.socialsecurity.gov/prescriptionhelp/.

State Assistance Programs

Many individual states offer help with prescription drugs through *State Pharmaceutical Assistance Programs* or *SPAPs*. Each state determines its own qualification limits. These limits are usually more lenient than those of federal programs so it may be easier to qualify for SPAPs. If you do qualify, you will also qualify for an SEP. This can allow you to make changes to your medical coverage outside of the AEP. If you're not happy with your Part D plan or would like to switch to a different Medicare Advantage Plan, you can makes changes as long as your current plan and your future plan both include Part D benefits. Remember that you can only use the SPAP SEP once each year. Below is a list of some state programs available. This list is not exhaustive so be sure to check your state's website for more information.

STATE	SPAP NAME	PHONE	WEB LINK
Colorado	Colorado Bridging the Gap	(303) 692-2783	http://www.cdphe.state.co.us/dc/HIVandSTD/ryanwhite/medicared.html
Connecticut	(PACE)	(800) 423-5026	http://www.connpace.com/
Delaware	Prescription Assistance Program (PDAP)	(800) 996-9969 EXT: 2	http://www.dhss.delaware.gov/dhss/dmma/dpap.html#print
Idaho	(IDAGAP)	(208) 334-5943	http://healthandwelfare.idaho.gov/Health/FamilyPlanningSTDHIV/HIVCareandTreatment/tabid/391/Default.aspx
Illinois	Illinois Cares Rx Plus	(800) 226-0768	http://www.illinoiscaresrx.com/
Indiana	HoosierRx	(866) 267-4679	http://www.in.gov/fssa/elderly/hoosierrx/
Massachusetts	Massachusetts Prescription Advantage	(800) 243-4636 EXT: 2	http://www.mass.gov/elders/healthcare/prescription-advantage/
Maryland	Senior Prescription Drug Assistance Program	(800) 551-5995	http://marylandspdap.com
Maine	Maine Low Cost Drugs for the Elderly or Disabled Program	(866) 796-2463	http://www.maine.gov/dhhs/beas/resource/lc_drugs.htm
Missouri	Missouri Rx Plan	(800) 375-1406	http://morx.mo.gov/
Montana	Montana Big Sky Rx Program	(866) 369-1233	http://www.dphhs.mt.gov/prescriptiondrug/bigsky.shtml
North Carolina	North Carolina HIV SPAP	(919) 733-7301	http://epi.publichealth.nc.gov/cd/hiv/adap.html
New Jersey	New Jersey Senior Gold	(800) 792-9745	http://www.state.nj.us/health/seniorbenefits/seniorgold.shtml
Nevada	Nevada Senior Rx Program	(866) 303-6323 (775) 687-4210	http://dhhs.nv.gov/SeniorRx.htm
New York	EPIC	(800) 332-3742	http://www.health.state.ny.us/nysdoh/epic/faq.htm
Pennsylvania	(PACE)	(717) 651-3600	http://www.aging.state.pa.us/portal/server.pt/community/pace_and_affordable_medications/17942
Texas	Texas Kidney Health Care Program (KHC)	(800) 222-3986	http://www.dshs.state.tx.us/kidney/default.shtm
Virginia	Virginia HIV SPAP	(800) 366-7741	http://www.vdh.virginia.gov/epidemiology/DiseasePrevention/spap.htm
U.S. Virgin Islands	U.S. Virgin Islands Senior Citizens Affairs Pharmaceutical Assistance	(340) 774-0930	http://www.dhs.gov.vi/seniors/pharmaceutical.html
Vermont	VPham	(800) 250-8427	http://www.greenmountaincare.org/vermont-health-insurance-plans/prescription-assistance
Washington	Washington State Health Insurance Pool	(800) 877-5187	https://www.wship.org/Default.asp
Wisconsin	Wisconsin SeniorCare	(800) 657-2038	http://www.dhs.wisconsin.gov/seniorcare/

Local Assistance

In addition to state and federal programs, there are also local programs for which you may be eligible. Most hospitals have financial assistance programs. Simply call your local hospital and speak with the finance department to find out more. If they have assistance programs, ask for details regarding qualification. Many pay a percentage of what's left after your insurance pays. Even if you qualify for only a 25 percent discount, the savings can add up quickly.

In addition to local providers, your local social services office may offer help. Some have access to other types of assistance programs. Many offer one-time help for specific items like medical bills or emergency fuel assistance. Also check with local churches. Some have benevolent funds that can be used to help with medical or prescription drug costs.

***

Here are a few tips concerning state and federal assistance programs that may be of particular interest to you as the consumer.

- Check federal assistance programs first. State and local programs will likely have less stringent qualification requirements.
- Check your state pharmaceutical programs next either using the list provided here or using information from your state's official website.
- Check with your local social services office.
- Lastly, check with local churches for other assistance programs.

CHAPTER TEN:

❖

Optimizing Your Medicare Benefits

Unfortunately, once you've successfully selected a Medicare plan, your work isn't completely finished. Unless you continue to maintain and optimize your benefits each year, you might not have the best plan fit. Here are a few simple things you should do on an annual basis in order to maximize your benefits.

Review Your ANOC

Probably the most important thing that you should do each year is read your plan's ANOC. This document provides all of the premium, cost-sharing, formulary, and provider changes that your current plan will undergo in the upcoming year. Read the ANOC for both your Part C plan as well as your Part D plan if they are not combined. Here's why. Let's say you join a plan and the cost sharing for a service is X. If you aren't paying attention and you use this service years later assuming that the cost will still be X, you could be surprised by a substantially higher bill.

Reading the ANOC is the only way to remain abreast of plan modifications. Plans can change significantly from year to year. I know that it can feel like reading a phone book, but most plans provide a concise outline at the beginning and then go into detail. You only need to read the outline to get a feel for the changes coming. If they don't seem too drastic and you're satisfied with your current coverage and service, then you don't need to do anything. If some of the changes directly affect the service categories that you use frequently, then you should see if an alternative plan would suit you better. If you find that the premiums or the benefits of your current plan don't line up with your needs, call your agent if you have one. Your agent is not a psychic. Unless you reach out, he or she won't know that you need help. If you don't have an agent or if your agent is unresponsive, go to http://medicareplanchoice.com and request a quote for a new plan. You can also call 800-332-7557 8:00 a.m. to 3:00 p.m. EST for support. I can help those that already have Medicare just as easily as those individuals who are getting started.

Review Your Explanation of Benefits

The second thing you should do is review your prior year's *explanation of benefits (EOB)* statements. Each time your plan pays a claim, the details of that claim are sent to you. The EOB will include how much was charged, how much was approved, how much was paid by the plan, and how much you're responsible for. Once you learn to read these summaries, you'll find most plans provide a total not only for the individual service but also for the year to date. You may even be able to see how much you paid in each category (e.g., medical equipment, treatments, or physical therapy). Your EOB will also show how much of the total out-of-pocket maximum you used during the year. If you attained the annual maximum out-of-pocket limit you should consider switching to a more comprehensive policy. The same is true if the amount you spent on medical service cost sharing was considerably higher than what the premium might be for a more comprehensive plan containing lower copay thresholds. This is especially the case if the services you used are services you expect to use frequently or if those services are required to keep your current health stable.

This step also applies to your Part D drug plan. Review each individual drug that you were prescribed as well as your total expenses. You might find that the majority of your costs were associated with just one or two prescriptions. If so, consider looking into generic brands. If that's not an option, shop formularies to see if another plan includes your brand as part of a lower tier level. Make sure that you take advantage of any federal, state, and/or local pharmacy plans that offer prescription savings.

Take some time to evaluate the overall effectiveness of your plan. Were the claims submitted on your behalf paid in a timely and accurate manner? Did you experience any difficulties with doctor availability? Did you receive prompt service from your agent when you had questions or service needs?

If you receive any type of assistance from federal, state, or local programs, make sure to do any necessary recertification. Many of these programs have annual or semiannual recertification requirements. If you do not recertify, you could be automatically dropped from the program. It's crucial to keep up. Additionally, income or marital changes could impact your status or even your eligibility. Keep up with these qualification requirements in order to maintain your status to participate in extra assistance programs.

Making the commitment to review your plan can help to ensure that you remain in the best plan for your personal circumstances. These simple steps can keep you from overspending on premiums and on cost-sharing amounts while maintaining your receipt of assistance from extra help programs. Though these steps take a little bit of work, they are well worth your time.

CHAPTER ELEVEN:

❖

The Value of an Agent

People often find themselves lacking the information that they need about a particular subject. In these instances, many consider hiring a professional to represent them in this unfamiliar field. Attorneys, accountants, and tax professionals come to mind right away. When there is simply too much to comprehend and too many rules and regulations to understand, it's often worth spending the money to hire an individual who already has the necessary insight. Doing so could save you time and money in the long run as you're able to avoid mistakes and unnecessary adjustments. Wouldn't it be nice to get this kind of help for free? Well, even though they say there's no such thing as a free lunch, there actually is. As an insurance professional, I spend long hours learning the ins and outs of the various policies. Every year I pursue product certifications and continuing education courses to satisfy my license requirements. This keeps me at the top of my game.

Did you know that most producer insurance professionals get paid by the companies that we represent rather than the clients who we serve? That's right. As a matter of fact, as a professional agent I do more to advise and protect my clients and to make sure that they remain satisfied than I do to sell policies. Producer insurance agents only get paid when their clients have a policy that is current. If a customer is not happy and drops one of my policies, that customer also terminates me as their agent. Therefore, I am always trying my best to make sure that my clients have the proper coverage so that if there is a claim, the policy will cover what was agreed upon. If my clients are satisfied, they will continue the policy. That keeps me employed. I've been helping Medicare-eligible individuals find the right plan for over fourteen years. I have thousands of satisfied clients who value the personal service that I offer.

Virtual Meetings

If you are not familiar with virtual meetings, allow me to describe how they work. Someone sends an e-mail containing a link to another person. The recipient of that e-mail then clicks on the link, which takes them to a virtual or online meeting place. There, the two parties can hold a private, confidential discussion. There is no need for special equipment, though you must have a high-speed Internet connection. Simply use the speakers and microphone in your computer or your telephone to communicate. There are no fees, memberships, or costs associated with this service. Virtual meetings provide a simple means to interact over long distances.

I used to drive all over, both in my state and beyond. Driving forty or fifty thousand miles a year was not unusual for me. This limited the number of people I could help. But thanks to this new technology, I am now in the position to offer my expertise to people farther away. This means that you have access to the benefits of my experience and insight for free. I will look over your health care needs to make sure that you select the plan that not only meets your medical needs but also your lifestyle including your budget. In addition, I will look at the various federal and state subsidy programs that might help you. To take advantage of this exclusive opportunity, go to Medicareplanchoice.com, click on web chat, and fill in your name, e-mail address, and other personal information. Submit your completed form including the date and time that you would like to meet. I will confirm the appointment or offer an alternate if I am otherwise booked. Once you are confirmed, you will receive an e-mail with a link to our private virtual meeting. We will discuss your situation to see if I can help you. There is no pressure and no hard close—I promise. I will simply provide you with the information that you need to make a wise decision concerning the Medicare plan that will fit you best.

Some people are under the impression that if they use the services of an agent, they will end up paying more than if they bought directly through an insurance company. This is not the case. The fact is that companies charge everyone equal premium amounts for Medicare policies issued, regardless of the involvement of a personal agent. Therefore, if you're not using an agent, you're losing out on the value that an agent brings to the table. I absolutely believe that I bring value to every client that I serve. This value can be broken down into three categories: knowledge, experience, and service.

Knowing the procedures that must be followed and the rules that apply in each situation is invaluable. A person who is not immersed in the health care insurance business on a daily basis simply cannot keep up with all of the rules and regulations. I've seen too many people make costly mistakes or choices with serious ramifications. I advise my clients in order to help them avoid such mistakes, thereby eliminating penalties, reducing out-of-pocket costs, and even averting loss of coverage. Every year I am faced with recertification testing and product qualifications so that I remain as knowledgeable as I can in all of these crucial areas.

An agent who is experienced has developed processes and procedures in order to correctly handle every situation. Knowing the marketplace can only come through daily experience and exposure. I strive to point you toward plans and resources that could benefit your situation while keeping you informed of any changes that might affect you in the future. There's nothing more frustrating than purchasing a product or service and having questions or requiring repairs for that product or service only to be directed to a call center or website that isn't helpful. Customer service seems to be turning into a thing of the past. I do otherwise. I recently took a call from one of my clients regarding an emergency visit claim. I made two phone calls and solved the issue in five minutes. My staff is also available to assist between 8:00 a.m. and 3:00 p.m. EST Monday through Friday. The bottom line is that an agent has more reason to solve issues quickly and to keep customers satisfied than any call center representative who gets paid to answer the phone. An agent only gets paid if he or she has current customers—happy customers. You have nothing to lose and everything to gain by taking advantage of the free services provided by an agent. Go to http://medicareplanchoice.com and request a quote or call my toll free line at 800-332-7557 to get started or to get your questions regarding Medicare benefits answered.

I hope that this book has proven to be a valuable asset in your Medicare decision-making process. I welcome your feedback regarding your personal experience. If you have any suggestions as to how this information could be improved or if you find any errors or omissions, please contact me through the contact page on my website. Finally, if you've experienced a pleasant or positive experience, please pass this material on to a friend or relative who require assistance with their own health care needs.

Receive FREE Coaching from the Author

Register at www.medicareplanchoice.com to receive a free thirty-minute coaching session with author Dan Brooks. This session will take place via web chat or by telephone in accordance with the author's schedule.

Access any of the resources below by registering at www.medicareplanchoice.com or by completing the form on the following page to receive any or all by mail (with $6.95 for shipping and handling).

1. "Avoid the Seven Most Common Mistakes to Enrolling in a Medicare Plan": Learn anywhere you can listen as Dan explains the secrets to avoiding common mistakes and provides hints for finding the right plan. (audio/CD)
2. "Medicare Basics": By viewing this DVD, you will have a well-rounded understanding of the different parts of Medicare. (video/DVD)
3. "Two Ways to Get Your Medicare": Understand the two fundamental choices you have with respect to Medicare plans. (video/DVD)
4. "Medicare Advantage": Learn about Part C, the types of plans available, and the rules that apply to each type. (video/DVD)
5. "Medicare Supplement": Discover what the different plans cover and which plan might provide the best value for you. (video/DVD)
6. "Medicare Part D": What is *the doughnut hole* and how can you avoid it? (video/DVD)

Receive FREE Coaching from the Author

Name_____
Address_____
City_____
State_____Zip:_____Phone_____
Fax_____Email:_____
Credit Card_____,Exp.Date:_____
Authorized signature for the shipping charge of $6.95
X_____
Must have information above. No PO boxes please. S&H covers one or all CD/DVDs)
Fax this order form to **801-697-5951** or **716-639-3325**
Make check or money order payable to Dan Brooks
Mail this completed form to 815 Town Line Rd. Johnson City, NY 13790
Please send me the following resources #'s _____ or ALL_____
Please check which of the following best describes your current situation:
__I will be eligible for Medicare in the next 3-6 months and will not have group insurance.
__I will be eligible for Medicare in the next 6-12 months and will not have group insurance.
__I will be eligible for Medicare this year but will continue working for _____ years.
__My company will continue my coverage as part of my retirement benefits.
__I have military or government insurance that I will rely on.
No phone orders will be accepted

Glossary

Affordable Care Act (ACA): Also known as "Obamacare", instituted mandatory medical coverage for individals. Tax credits and premium assistance is given based upon income.

Age Issue: One of the underwriting methods used by insurance companies to price Medigap policies.

Annual Election Period (AEP): A period that runs from October 15 to December 7 each year, during which you can make changes and adjustments to your Medicare benefits.

Annual Notice of Change (ANOC): Sent in October by Medicare Advantage and PDP plans, this notice discloses premium, co-pay, coinsurance, and formulary changes for the upcoming year.

Appeals Process: The action you can take if you disagree with a coverage or payment decision made by Medicare, Medicare Advantage, or a PDP.

Attained-Age Rated: One of the underwriting methods used by insurance companies to price Medigap policies.

Basic Benefits: The minimum threshold of coverage to designate a standard Medicare supplement or Medigap policy.

Benefit Period: The way in which Original Medicare measures your use of hospital and skilled nursing facility services.

Catastrophic Coverage: Stage four of a Medicare PDP, during which the patient pays the greater of 5 percent coinsurance or $2.65 co-pay for generic and $6.60 co-pay for brand-name drugs.

Chronic Health Condition: A health condition or disease that is persistent or has long-lasting effects and typically requires ongoing management or treatment.

Coinsurance: Cost sharing of medical or prescription bills usually based on a percentage.

Community Rated: One of the underwriting methods used by insurance companies to price Medigap policies.

Consolidated Omnibus Budget Reconciliation Act (COBRA): Act that allows employees to temporarily keep employer health insurance benefits after employment ends or after loss of coverage from a spousal employer.

Contracted Physician: A physician who has agreed to the terms and conditions of a Medicare health plan.

Co-payment: Cost sharing of medical or prescription bills usually based on a fixed fee.

Creditable Coverage: Prescription drug coverage that is at least equal to or greater than the benchmark Medicare Part D PDP.

Deductible: The amount that must be paid prior to insurance cost sharing.

Doughnut Hole: Also known as a coverage gap, stage three of a Medicare Part D plan involving a lack of coverage. Coverage begins again during stage four, the catastrophic phase.

Drug Tiers: The cost sharing levels for drugs covered by Part D plans.

Durable Medical Equipment (DME): Medical equipment used in the home to aid in a better quality of living. Common examples are wheelchairs, nebulizers, and oxygen machines.

Election Period: A set time during which changes or adjustments can be made to one's Medicare benefits.

Employer Group Health Plan (EGHP):- A group health insurance policy administered by an employer

End-Stage Renal Disease (ESRD):- A disease where the kidneys stop working well enough to live without dialysis or a transplant.

Entry-Age Rated: One of the underwriting methods used by insurance companies to price Medigap policies.

Evidence of Coverage: The document used to detail plan benefits and cost sharing in a Medicare Advantage or Medicare Part D plan.

Explanation of Benefits (EOB): Also known as a summary of benefits, details individual claims as to the amount charged, the amount approved, the amount paid by insurance, and the member responsibility amount

Extra Help: A Medicare program intended to help people with limited income and limited resources pay Medicare prescription drug costs.

Formulary: The unique list of drugs covered by each Medicare Part D plan sponsor.

Glossary

General Enrollment Period: A Medicare election period (January 1 to March 31) during which anyone eligible for Medicare can enroll.

Guaranteed Issue: A situation wherein a policy is offered to any eligible applicant regardless of preexisting health conditions.

Health Maintenance Organization (HMO): A type of Medicare Advantage Plan.

Home Health Care: A Part A Medicare benefit. The receipt thereof must be medically necessary and can include skilled nursing services and physical therapy provided by a Medicare-certified home health agency.

Hospice: A Medicare benefit for those who are determined to be terminally ill.

Income Related Monthly Adjustment Amount (IRMAA): An additional amount added to your Part D premium due to higher levels of income reported in the prior two years.

Initial Coverage Election Period (ICEP): Allows you to initiate your Medicare coverage. You can apply during the three months before, the month of or during the three months directly following your sixty-fifth birthday.

Late Enrollment Penalty (LEP): A penalty that can be applied if Medicare Part B or Part D is not taken when you're initially eligible.

Lifetime Reserve Days: Extended hospital stays between 91 and 150 covered under Part A Medicare. These days can be used only once in a given lifetime.

Maximum Out-of-Pocket Limit: The maximum one can spend on covered medical services during the calendar year. This applies to both Medicare supplement and Medicare Advantage policies. Once met, the policy will pay 100 percent of covered services for the remainder of year.

Medicaid: State-sponsored medical assistance that is income and resource sensitive.

Medical Savings Account (MSA): A form of Medicare Advantage that uses an insurance policy with a high deductible combined with a savings account.

Medicare Advantage: Also referred to as Part C Medicare, private plans that administer Part A, Part B, and Part D Medicare benefits. They operate under HMO, PPO, PFFS, and SNP formats. Medicare Advantage reflects one of the two ways in which one can accept Medicare benefits.

Medicare Advantage Disenrollment Period (MADP): An annual election period (January 1 through February 14) during which one can leave a Medicare Advantage Plan and revert back to Original Medicare benefits.

Medicare Part A: Hospital coverage under the Original Medicare program.

Medicare Part B: Medical coverage under the Original Medicare program.

Medicare Part C: Also known as Medicare Advantage, private insurance companies that administer Part A, Part B, and Part D benefits.

Medicare Part D: The prescription drug portion of the Medicare program.

Medicare Supplement Policy: A private insurance policy that supplements Original Medicare claims payments.

Medigap: A Medicare supplement policy.

Original Medicare: The standard parts of the Original Medicare system or Part A (hospital) and Part B (medical).

Out of Network: Receiving services from a provider that is not contracted with the Medicare plan in which one is enrolled, often resulting in a higher cost-sharing portion.

Participating Provider: A provider that is contracted with a Medicare Advantage Plan and is considered to be in network.

Point-of-Service (POS): A plan in which patients can see providers who are out of the network. There may be limits for usage and higher cost-sharing portions.

Preferred Provider Organization (PPO): A type of Medicare Advantage or Part C plan that includes a network of doctors and hospitals. Plan members can go out of network, usually with higher cost sharing.

Prescription Drug Plan (PDP): A stand-alone Part D prescription drug plan.

Primary Care Physician (PCP): A physician who usually provides first contact for a person with an undiagnosed health concern. Can also help coordinate care by referring patients to other doctors for specialized care.

Primary Payer: The insurance that pays first when coordinating payments with a Medicare plan.

Prior Authorization: A restriction placed on certain drugs by some Part D plans that require the patient or the patient's doctor to get preauthorization before filling a prescription.

Glossary

Private Fee-for-Service (PFFS): A type of Medicare Advantage or Part C plan in which one can go to any doctor or hospital that will accept the plan's terms and conditions.

Qualified Disabled and Working Individuals (QDWI): A program qualification that stipulates a individual can receive assistance with Part A premiums if he or she is able to meet the income and resource guidelines set forth in that state.

Qualifying Individual (QI): A program qualification that stipulates an individual can receive assistance with premiums if he or she is able to meet the income and resource guidelines set forth in that state.

Qualified Medicare Beneficiary (QMB): A program qualification that stipulates a n individual can receive assistance with premiums, deductibles, coinsurances, and co-payments if he or she is able to meet the income and resource guidelines set forth in that state.

Quantity Limits: A restriction placed on certain drugs by Part D plans that limits the quantity of pills or tablets that can be filled in a month's supply.

Secondary Payer: The insurance that pays second when coordinating payments with a Medicare plan.

Special Election Period (SEP): An election period that can be used at any time during the year to make changes to one's Medicare benefits.

Specified Low-Income Medicare Beneficiary (SLMB): A program qualification that stipulates an individual can receive help with Part B premiums if he or she is able to meet the income and resource guidelines set forth in that state.

State Pharmaceutical Assistance Program (SPAP): State funded programs designed to assist individuals with costs associated with Part D Medicare.

Step Therapy: A restriction placed on certain drugs by Part D plans that requires patients to try other drugs in a given treatment class before receiving the first drug requested.

Summary of Benefits: A document that details plan benefits and cost sharing in a Medicare Advantage or Medicare Part D plan.

Usual and Customary: A term used by insurance companies to represent an acceptable payment amount for a certain service that was provided to the member.

Made in the USA
San Bernardino, CA
31 August 2014